THE FISH HAVE MOVED

THEODUS DRAKE

ISBN: 978-1-5356-0649-3

This book is dedicated to my father and my mother, the late, Theodus and Sarah Drake who were always there insisting that we (their children) give their best to Christ. To my wife Carrie who has been an incredible partner in ministry for over thirty years. To the wonderful people at the Second Mt Zion Baptist Church in Albany, Georgia who have provided so much encouragement and support for over twenty-two years.

CONTENTS

Foreword

MOST BIBLE READERS WILL AGREE that to study the life and teachings of Jesus Christ is to study the life and works of a man that understood the times in which He lived. The parables He used, the methodology he employed as He interacted with people, and the appropriateness of His language all point to the fact that He could connect with people because He understood the times in which He lived, and therefore could contextualize His message in a way that allowed Him to achieve His desired outcome.

One of the challenges facing local churches today - especially churches that have existed for a long period of time - is determining how we do ministry in a culture that is ever-changing. One thing that is obvious by the decline or plateauing of so many churches is that we have not done a good job of adjusting so that we can contextualize the gospel message and methodology to be impactful in the culture in which we do ministry. *We have been called to be 'fishers of men'*. The test of our success is the answer to the question, *"Have we caught any fish?"*

In his thought-provoking book, *"The Fish Have Moved"* Pastor Theodus Drake offers sage wisdom for anyone who is involved in ministry as well as anyone who is concerned about the capacity of the church to *'serve this present age'*. His life experiences growing up intimately involved the life of the church at every level of membership and leadership. His 30 plus years of pastoral leadership, his involvement in the denominational work in the GMBC of Georgia Pastor's Conference, along with his analysis of research data qualify him to speak on this subject.

The information he presents in his book is easy to follow and easy to implement. In a very powerful way, Pastor Drake uses his experiences as a fisherman to help us understand how *we the church* are to be fishers of men. I've been in ministry for more than 30 years, and it is true that – while the Gospel has remained the same – the fish have moved, and the bait or methodology of reaching the fish has changed. Pastor Drake helps us to understand what these changes are and offers us a framework by which to examine our ministries so we can improve our capacity to execute the Great Commission and the Great Commandment.

Our goal as the church is not to maintain the status quo but to transform the world through the person and works of Jesus Christ. *Let's commit ourselves to being the best fishers of men we can be.*

Daniel B. Simmons, Senior Pastor
Mount Zion Baptist Church
Albany, GA

The Fish Have Moved

Introduction

I GREW UP IN SOUTH Georgia in a small rural community where we spent a great deal of time in church. My parents had fourteen children and we were all very active in our home church and in the church community. My parents were church leaders and most of my brothers and sisters were very gifted musicians and vocalists. Our home church, with approximately seventy-five members, provided the stage for our church involvement and helped us form our church theology. It was there that we learned the basic tenets of the Christian faith. Out of my parents' fourteen children seven became licensed ministers and five of them became pastors. Most of the perspectives that are put forth in this book have come from the limited knowledge that I have acquired as a busy pastor who has sought to maintain a relative ministry for the present age and the experience of over fifty years of active church leadership, first in Youth Ministry and subsequently in Adult Ministry. Although much of the content of this book has been my observations for several years, I felt that I did not have the in-depth expertise to publish it. Through the encouragement and continuous nudging of my friend and fellow pastor Lawrence Knighton, I set out to do it. While much of what is in the book is based on perspectives and experiences, rather than academics or in-depth research, it is my hope that it will generate thought and conversation. More so, I hope it will provide a fresh look at where the church is today, in the context of the age she serves and what imperatives we face today as church leaders. In rural South Georgia, those churches that were scattered throughout the country side, serving as faith centers for rural families, are near extinction. Will they survive past the next generation? Should they survive? How can they survive? What is needed for them to survive? These are questions facing our parents' church today.

The Fish Have Moved

So it was, as the multitude pressed about Him to hear the word of God, that He stood by the Lake of Gennesaret, ² and saw two boats standing by the lake; but the fishermen had gone from them and were washing their nets. ³ Then He got into one of the boats, which was Simon's, and asked him to put out a little from the land. And He sat down and taught the multitudes from the boat. ⁴ When He had stopped speaking, He said to Simon, "Launch out into the deep and let down your nets for a catch." ⁵ But Simon answered and said to Him, "Master, we have toiled all night and caught nothing; nevertheless at Your word I will let down the net." ⁶ And when they had done this, they caught a great number of fish, and their net was breaking. ⁷ So they signaled to their partners in the other boat to come and help them. And they came and filled both the boats, so that they began to sink. ⁸ When Simon Peter saw it, he fell down at Jesus' knees, saying, "Depart from me, for I am a sinful man, O Lord!" ⁹ For he and all who were with him were astonished at the catch of fish which they had taken; ¹⁰ and so also were James and John, the sons of Zebedee, who were partners with Simon. And Jesus said to Simon, "Do not be afraid. From now on you will catch men." (Luke 5:1-10)

Chapter 1

THE FISH HAVE MOVED

IT WAS DURING CRAPPIE SEASON, early spring when the crappie fish invade shallow-waters to lay their eggs during the spring spawning season.

Every year about the same time we had come to our favorite shallow-water location and for years, had caught the maximum limit of fish that the game and Fish Commission laws allowed. And so, we came with great expectations and with great investment; proven bait and tackle, tackle box filled with alternatives, choices and extras, coolers filled with ice, live wells running with aerator- circulating water and high-wattage lights for the night. It was a sure thing. But something was not right. They were not biting like they normally do. Well, "be patient," we said. "They will bite after a while." And so we mustered a little patience and dug in. After about seven hours of waiting and watching, around 2AM in the morning, we decided to give it up...to go home...yes, to call it quits.

This particular fishing trip had not been productive. After traveling nearly a hundred miles and spending a considerable amount of money for the trip's accessories, we surrendered to failure and began our disappointing journey to the docks. As we headed out we passed by a man headed in the opposite direction and, with a friendly tip, I shouted out, "They ain't biting!" He shouted back, "They have gone back to the deep waters." So this is why we have not caught any fish. They have moved.

We had come a long way to fish. We had invested a lot of time, effort and resources toward this venture. We rented a cabin for three days. We bought a lot of food and snacks, not to mention the many other items that go along with a fishing trip. We had to make a decision about what we would do. We had three choices. 1. Continue to fish in shallow waters. 2. Cut the trip short, pack everything up, forfeit the cost of the cabin rental and go home; or 3. We could go out into the deep where the fish had gone.

The last option seemed to be the most sensible one. However, there was a problem with going to the deep. In fact, there were multiple problems with #3. We were not rigged for deep-water fishing. The fishing gear was rigged for shallow-water fishing. The ropes on our anchors were too short. The anchors were not heavy enough for fishing out into the open lake. The shallow waters were up in the sloughs bordered by trees. These trees blocked the strong winds during the windy season in the night. To go out into the open lake, in the dark, where there were no trees to block the strong winds, with the light-weight anchors that we had to secure the boat with, it would have been a disaster. And to top that off, we had an individual on the boat that was afraid of deep water.

Luke 5

Perhaps this was a similar situation that Peter, James, and John found themselves in Luke, Chapter 5. They too had been fishing…Yes! ALL NIGHT! And, they too "caught nothing!"

Dealing with failure, frustration, futility and fatigue, they had to make the disappointing decision to quit; to throw in the towel; to go home. These were experienced fishermen. They made their living fishing. They had been to fishing-school. They had made the proper investment. They had acquired all the accessories, bait and tackle needed for professional fishing. They had even invested in the big-tickets items; two boats. Using their proven skills, relying on their experience and using what every fisherman must have; a healthy quantity of patient, their efforts were still futile. Even the most steadfast fisherman will realize, even with a lot of patience and the right tackle and bait, there comes the time when you have to fold the nets. And so they did. They had fished all night and caught nothing. It was time to fold the net.

As the day began to dawn, the morning dew is dissipating in the morning sun, they cannot wait to put this night behind them. They now only wanted a place where they can rest, sleep, and forget. Just a small distance away, Jesus has brought his teaching ministry down to lakeside. The multitude is gathered around the shores to hear His teaching. As He is speaking to the crowd nearby, Jesus sees the struggling fishermen in their failure, washing their nets, with their boats anchored in the shallow waters. With the crowd pressing upon Him, His feet are in the water. A boat sitting in the shallow water near the shore would be a perfect platform to speak to the crowd. So, He borrows one of their boats to use as a platform to speak to the multitude and when He has finished teaching, He says to them, "Launch out into the deep and let down your nets for a catch!" We can be sure He has asked them the same question He asked them in John 21:5, "Have You Caught Anything"?

It is here that we can see how human and divine partnership can bring incredible results to what ordinarily would be futile. They could have responded so many ways. We are fishermen! We know how to fish! We have the experience! We have used the proven techniques! We have been doing it this way for years! This is how we were taught to do it! The problem with these responses is the results. "We have toiled all night – Nothing! Zero! Zilch!

> *"Master, we have toiled all night and caught nothing; nevertheless at Your word I will let down the net."* (Luke 5:5)

Can you recall times when your efforts were futile? After giving so much of your time, efforts, and resources with great expectations, you were disappointed at the outcome? A failed marriage, a child who became a prodigal, a business you started, a financial investment, a child you mentored, a relationship you nurtured, came to a failure. There is always a sense of weariness and downcastness that follow these kinds of experiences. After giving it all you had and you failed, to turn around and go back to something that has exhausted all you had to put into and it yielded you nothing, takes a lot of doing.

Thank God Peter had the humility and faith to say, "nevertheless." Nevertheless is a word that every believer should have in his mouth when he is in the presence of Jesus. Nevertheless is how the saints ought to respond to his own proven method when God says to do something different. Nevertheless is the acquiescing of my will to His Will. Nevertheless is how we treat our know-how to God's Omniscience. Nevertheless is how the saints transition from personal failures to Divine guidance.

Nevertheless is how we say to God, "I hear You, God." Nevertheless is the same as Proverbs 3:5 *Trust in the Lord with all of your heart and lean not on your own understanding. In all of your doings, acknowledge Him and He will direct your way.*

Nevertheless, I will not doubt your Word. Nevertheless, I will not question Your Power. Nevertheless, I will not challenge Your Authority. Nevertheless, I will leave the futility of these shallow waters where my efforts have not been productive, launch out into the deep waters and let down my net. I will do it because You say do it.

> *And when they had done this, they caught a great number of fish, and their net was breaking. (Luke 5:7)*

Amazingly, they did not have to change boats. They did not have to get new people. They did not have to go to the fish-and-bait and tackle store to get new tackle. They simply moved. They moved because the Fish had moved.

Perhaps in these fish stories there are some powerful allegories and metaphors that might uncover some realities of the Church today. Jesus, Himself used this story metaphorically when He said, *"Do not be afraid. From now on you will catch men." (Luke 5:10).*

"Fishermen of men" are who we are. As individual disciples of Christ, as an institution and as a body of believers, our primary responsibility is to go out and catch men for the Kingdom of God. When we as the Church walk away from this responsibility, we essentially lose our authenticity. We are relegated to social clubs and organizations whose only purpose is to serve each other. There is no argument here. The great majority of Christianity confirms this in their teaching and in their talk. Yet we can easily see that the church is losing its grips on those who call themselves believers and its power to bring sinners to Christ. Most churches will check "yes," if asked, "Is evangelism a priority for your church?" Yet the number of people who are being saved is rapidly declining. Perhaps the real problem of most churches today is not that they do not see evangelism as a priority, it may be that the kind of evangelism they are doing is not productive. And, as a result, even with their best efforts, their pews are getting progressively empty. Their memberships are steadily declining. Regardless of what most churches response is when asked, "Is evangelism a priority for your church?" the truth is that most churches have given up on the Ministry of Evangelism.

In his book, Boiling Point, George Barna writes,

> "The Great Commission clearly commands Christians to share the good news about Jesus' life,

death and atoning resurrection with the world. But in a relativistic society, such a challenge is less inspiring and meaningful. In fact, for many people, including tens of millions of devoted Christians, evangelism is dismissed because it is both counterculture and optional. In a culture in which there is no absolute moral truth, the Bible is not a definitive source of guidance for behavior. Its exhortations to strategically share the Christian faith with non-believers are seen as well-intentioned but un-motivating demands."[1]

With the society in which we live continuously moving towards a secular society, even those who call themselves Christians do not see the need to make evangelism a priority for the Church.

We may say that evangelism is a priority, but there is evidence to the contrary. Jesus declared, "*For where your treasure is, there your heart will be also.*"[2] In modern day interpretation, "If you want to know the most important ministry in a church, examine the budget and financials." The "money where your mouth is" rule may not apply.

Why have many churches given up on the very thing that gives them legitimacy and authenticity? Could it be because the investment does not produce the expected dividends? It may be that the efforts too often end in futility. I was talking to a pastor who led a number of people in his congregation to evangelize the community around their church. Their Saturday efforts resulted in single digit converts. Only 50% of them showed up for baptism and with those who were baptized, it has taken more efforts to keep them than get them. Some of them cannot even be found.

Is it time to reexamine our evangelistic methods? How do we serve the good news to a world that feels like it does not need to hear it?

In the 50s and 60's, when I grew up, the people within the community were mostly related to one another by religion. Churches of the community were so closely associated with one another that, even though our membership church only met once a month, we were in church practically every Sunday. During the revival seasons (May-September), much effort was focused on the un-churched to get them in on the mourners' bench to get them saved and baptized. Baptism mostly occurred during the summer months, with the exception of perhaps a few city churches that had the ability to heat the baptismal water. During the summer, in open ponds, creeks and pools built for baptism, hundreds of new converts would be ushered into the faith. Families and the community would actively track potential candidates for conversion and give prayerful attention to them. Prayer Warriors would form partnerships to focus on those who had been on the mourner's bench for more than one revival season.

The church would spend an entire week in prayer for the salvation of those who had been guided to the Mourners' bench, and preach to them another week. After two weeks of prayer, testimonies, preaching and praise, the revival would end with a large number of new converts going to the water. The converts were dressed in white and were led down into the water. On that following Sunday, a great celebration of worship would occur when the newly converted saints would receive the right-hand-of-welcome. Others churches and the community would be invited to a big-day celebration where activities would take up a whole day with a big outdoor festival, feasting from the food-boxes of all the families of the church. People would come from miles around. Many who had moved north during the great migration would come home to the Homecoming Big-Day celebration. Cars would be parked everywhere. Many walked for miles. The singing and preaching was done mostly by uneducated church leaders who did not have much formal academic training. Quite often, they would testify that you do not need to go to school to be a preacher or a witness or to be anointed. And so, their sermons and teaching were not deep. No great theological depth. No skills in hermeneutics. No biblical apologetics. No thorough exegesis. No sensible logos. Not much importance on ethos, and a whole lot of attention to pathos. They worked on the emotions. And the sinners did come, in great numbers. Fast forward forty-fifty years later and the large number of sinners who came in out of the sinful world during revival time are not there anymore. The revivals have gone from two weeks to two and three nights and rarely do they produce multiple converts.

Today many of those same churches are gone. Many have plenty of empty seats and some have only one generation before they will have to close their doors. And it is not because there are fewer sinners to evangelize. It is because demographics and geographies have changed and cultures have shifted. The large number of people who lived in rural areas has now shifted to cities and urban areas. People have become more educated. Living conditions and standards for many have improved. Churches that once sat in the heart of a community now stand alone, isolated from large condensed populations. Furthermore, the importance of religion in the lives of many young people is much less than it was in the old days. In a 2010 study by the Pew research center, it was found that Americans ages 18 to 29 are considerably less religious than older Americans. Fewer young adults belong to any particular faith than older people do today. They also are less likely to be affiliated with a church than their parents' and grandparents' generations were when they were young. Fully one-in-four members of the millennial generation – so called because they were born after 1980 and began to come of age around the year 2000 – are unaffiliated with any particular faith. Indeed, millennials are significantly more unaffiliated than members of Generation X were at a comparable point in their life cycle (20% in the late 1990s) and twice as unaffiliated as Baby Boomers were as young adults (13% in the late 1970s). Young adults also attend religious services less often than older Americans today. And compared with their elders today, fewer young people say that religion is very important in their lives. Compared with their elders today, young people are much less likely to affiliate with any religious tradition or to identify themselves as part of a Christian denomination. Fully one-in-four adults under age 30 (25%) are unaffiliated, describing their religion as "atheist," "agnostic" or "nothing in particular." This compares with less than one-fifth of people in their 30s (19%), 15% of those in their 40s, 14% of those in their 50s and 10% or less among those 60 and older. About two-thirds of young people (68%) say they are members of a Christian denomination and 43% describe themselves as Protestants, compared with 81% of adults ages 30 and older who associate with Christian faiths and 53% who are Protestants.[3]

Because the Church has not reacted to these shifts with seriousness, it is losing its grip on society. The church seems to be losing its ability to catch fish. Is this something that we should accept? Is it a reality that we cannot do anything about? Should we just accept, adjust and move on with what we have, like downsizing, merging and/or consolidating? Or, should we acknowledge that the fish have moved to the deep and begin to look at retooling our ministries for deep water fishing? The only other options are to continue to fish in the shallowness of tradition and the past and continue in evangelistic futility, or we can just close our doors and quit. One thing I do know about being a fisherman, every true fisherman wants to catch fish.

On that fishing trip, we did not go home. We spent the next day retooling our fishing equipment for deep water fishing. And we launched out into the deep. We found the fish and we caught plenty of them. We were delayed but not unsuccessful. Now we can fish year-round. We don't have to wait until the spring spawning season when the crappies come to visit shallow waters. We can launch out into the deep where they live all the time. We can be successful in the deep. Why? Because we had the wisdom to see the futility of fishing where there are no fish, the ear to hear a voice from a distant boat telling us where the fish had gone, the vision to retool and the courage to go to the dangerous-deep.

When we decided that we would retool and go to the deep, we never once considered using a different kind of bait. Jigs and minnows are the bait for crappie. I never caught a crappie fish with a worm or cricket. The retooling we did was with the tackle; the tools --- longer fish lines, longer ropes on our anchors, heavier anchors, wind drags and life jackets.

When the Christian evangelists move from shallow water fishing to deep water fishing, there must be a retooling process as well. No, not in the changing of the bait (Gospel) but changing the tackle. Everything we do as a Church must be part of the retooling process, beginning with our preaching and our teaching.

When I was a young boy attending a revival, I remember one night the preacher preached the sermon made popular by the British theologian, Jonathan Edwards, "Sinners in the hands of an Angry God." He vividly described a graphic illustration of a sinner dangling from God's Hand, over an open flame. The preacher strongly proclaimed that this is what will happen to those who do not repent and be saved. That did it! When the invitation to discipleship was extended that night, everybody on the mourners' bench came off. Everyone thought their crying was in jubilation for being saved. They may have just been scared off the bench. It didn't take much theological effort to get those sinners to move. Just a little dramatized creativity associated with the bible about getting burned up in fire that was seventy-seven times hotter than the fire we know, and an offer of security by just coming forward. That did it. Today that same sermon might be amusing and annoying rather than provocative. Today the non-believers would perhaps challenge this theology with their own brand, contending instead that hell-fire is simply a metaphor of the grave or something.

We need to retool. We need to develop longer lines of inspiration rather than the short lines of provocation.

We need to use luring words like Love, Peace, Joy and Forgiveness rather than fire and brimstone. We need to replace the short lines of intolerance and exclusion with the long lines of tolerance and inclusion. We need to illuminate the light of grace by showing how God loves us all in spite of and regardless of. This is what the grace of God did for us. His patience was not short with us. His grace was not limited when we were saved. He waited long for us to come out of the world. He gave us second chances. He defended us when we were guilty. He looked beyond our faults.

Doing this without crossing the lines of holiness and righteousness will take different approaches than the ways we have evangelized in the past. However, these are the lures that the modern- day fish hunger for. For the church, particularly the church that is in the grips of tradition, this can be deep and dangerous.

In David Platt's book, "Counter Culture," he writes, "Everywhere we turn, battle lines are being drawn --- traditional marriages vs. gay marriage, pro-life vs. pro-choice, personal freedom vs. government protection. Seemly overnight, culture has shifted to the point where right and wrong are no longer measured by universal truth but by popular opinion. And as difficult conversations about homosexuality, abortion, and religious liberty continue to inject themselves into our workplaces, our churches, our schools and our homes,

Christians everywhere are asking: How are we supposed to respond to all this?"[4] What they are really saying is that the evangelistic and apologetic systems that the Church has been using in the past are inadequate for addressing the societal issues that face Christianity today. They are really saying that most of us Christians would find ourselves uncomfortable, uncertain and insecure when we are faced with discussions with non-Christians about these things. In most cases, when discussions do occur, most Christians will adversely misrepresent Jesus and His teachings and potential believers will not bite. The deep water evangelistic fisherman must be able to master God's Word (the Tools) in Deep water if we are to continue to be successful in evangelistic fishing.

In 2 Timothy, chapter 3:1-5, the Apostle Paul wrote to Timothy,

> [1] *This know also, that in the last days perilous times shall come.* [2] *For men shall be lovers of their own selves, covetous, boasters, proud, blasphemers, disobedient to parents, unthankful, unholy,* [3] *Without natural affection, trucebreakers, false accusers, incontinent, fierce, despisers of those that are good,* [4] *Traitors, heady, highminded, lovers of pleasures more than lovers of God;* [5] *Having a form of godliness, but denying the power thereof: from such turn away.*

This is the kind of culture the church faces today. These are deep water issues for the church and without re-tooling, the traditional church is headed for futile outcomes. "The Fish Have Moved."

As evangelistic fishermen, it is time that we consider doing what we did on that fishing trip. Maybe it's time that we consider retooling our approaches, our applications and our processes.

Romans 5:6-11

For when we were still without strength, in due time Christ died for the ungodly. [7] For scarcely for a righteous man will one die; yet perhaps for a good man someone would even dare to die. [8] But God demonstrates His own love toward us, in that while we were still sinners, Christ died for us. [9] Much more then, having now been justified by His blood, we shall be saved from wrath through Him. [10] For if when we were enemies we were reconciled to God through the death of His Son, much more, having been reconciled, we shall be saved by His life. [11] And not only that, but we also rejoice in God through our Lord Jesus Christ, through whom we have now received the reconciliation.

Chapter 2

Have You Caught Anything?

There is this place up at Lake Blackshear where we go fishing. For the past two years, every time I have gone to Lake Blackshear I headed to this place. The last ten times I have gone there to fish, I have wasted time. They just did not bite there for me anymore. I asked myself the last time I was there, "Why do you keep coming back to this place?" Here is the answer, "Because I used to catch a lot of fish here." I used to!

About a month ago I went up to Lake Blackshear and this time I decided enough is enough. Just around the corner from that spot is where I threw in. It took a minute but there they were. They had moved from just around the corner. I did not have to change lakes or find another boat. I did not even go very far. Just around the corner. I just came to grips with the futility of going back to that long-gone glory-hole that was once so productive but now all the fish are gone.

I do not know what made them move. It could have been the water temperature. It could have been the food source It could have been social change, or perhaps safety from alligators or other predator fish. Maybe there was a change in the lake's water level. The fact is the fish were not there anymore. The sooner I accepted that the sooner I could make the necessary shift and move on.

Every church ought to have periodic evaluations of its ministries, methodologies, modalities, leadership and structures. From evaluating cultures, current ministries, social trends, leadership makeup to accessing facilities, capacity and resources; every aspect of our operations should be examined for relevance and effectiveness. The pivoting and initiating question should be, "Have you caught anything?" Our decisions should not be determined by "what we used to do." I believe that the greatest hindrance to the great commission today is Yesterday. If we can just break free of Yesterday, if we can just stop Yesterday from dictating to us what we do today, we might be able to be productive. I am not suggesting that we forget what we learned yesterday. But what I am saying is that "unto everything there is a season" and maybe the reason why we are not catching any fish is because the shallow water season is over and the fish have gone to the deep.

I heard a preacher the other day, use Matt. 19:20 for a consolation for low attendance, *"For where two or three are gathered together in my name, there am I in the midst of them.* Jesus did not intend for this to be a consolation prize for an empty church. In fact, everywhere Jesus went, one word followed Him, "Multitude." This is not to say we ought not to feel no less worthy of Jesus' presence when we are few in numbers. But it is to say, we should not ignore our evangelistic problems and using this as an excuse.

"Have You Caught Anything?" Is what you are doing productive for the Kingdom? Is the way you are doing ministry bringing sinners to Christ or are you stuck in the way "we used to do it?" Are you fishing in the same place you fished in forty and fifty years ago? Have you Caught Anything?

What are you Fishing for?

Some years ago a couple of friends of ours joined us on a house boat for three days on the St. John River at Deland, Florida. We were anxious to catch some of those shell crackers that we saw in the cooler of the fisherman at the boat dock. When we saw them we were more anxious to get started. We were certain that we would have the same luck as that fisherman had. Hurriedly we made our way to what appeared to be a perfect place to do some damage. We had rented this large house boat that made it easy and comfortable to fish, converse and (more especially) brag. But they were not biting. At least they were not biting our bait. After spending a futile day in disappointment we shut down for the night. The next day we were back at it, doing the same thing. We caught nothing. After a while we lost our passion to fish. The large house boat had decks so we spent the next morning sitting in the easy chairs grilling and talking on one of the decks. Then this elderly gentleman in a very small john-boat anchored near us and as fast as he could get his bait in the water, he was pulling them up. We asked him, "What are you fishing with?" He said, "Little reds." So that's what they are biting. All this time, coming all this way, with this big ole house boat, our success rested on "little reds." Worms! Well, let's weigh anchor and go get some; "little reds." We did and sure enough, we caught fish. We were so sure of our bait (crickets and pond worms) that we never thought we had a bait problem. The tragedy was, it was time to turn in the boat. We had only three days and two and half of them had gone by before we discovered that we had the wrong bait. If only we had inquired at the dock to the man with the cooler full of fish we might have come home with plenty of fish and plenty of fish testimonies. He lived in the areas. He was familiar with the river. He knew where the fish hung out and what they were biting.

There are some churches that are still catching plenty of fish. My friend Pastor Daniel Simmons, Pastor of the

Mt Zion Baptist Church in Albany, Georgia, just two miles from our church asked to borrow some baptismal gowns one Saturday. They had sixty new converts to baptize. One hundred had joined. For me, that's a cooler full. Maybe all of us need to ask him, "What are you fishing with?" Was it pride that did not allow us to ask the man at the boat-dock? Was it envy? Was it that we did not need his secret because we had our own? Was it that his ethnicity was different than ours? I do not know. But not asking cost us.

Luke 5:6-7 KJVS

[6] And when they had this done, they enclosed a great multitude of fishes: and their net brake. [7] And they beckoned unto their partners, which were in the other ship, that they should come and help them. And they came, and filled both the ships, so that they began to sink.

The other fishermen gained from the overflow. They did not gaze in envy; they came and joined the success. AND...The nets were still spilling over. Perhaps if the ecclesiastical fishermen would join together in the place where the fish have moved, there would not be as many little boats who are struggling to stay on the water. The fish have moved. It is time for shifting.

Some argue, the Church should not change because the world is changing. The church should not change to accommodate a shifting and deteriorating society. They say, "There is nothing different about God. He changes not." *Hebrews 13:8 KJVS Jesus Christ the same yesterday, and today, and forever.*

Any Christian with the proper theological interpretation cannot argue the fact that God does not change. However, people do change and the challenge for the modern-day evangelist is to know how to take this unchangeable God and offer Him to a changed people. How do we take the immutable gospel and minister to a changing world?

One of the classic pieces of Christian literature is a timeless small book by J. B. Phillips entitled, "Your God is too small."[5] Essentially, Phillips contends that if your God fits only into your culture, your theology, your denomination, your tradition, your God is too small. God is a transcending God. He is too great a God to be contained into one little human theology. He is too big a God to be contained into a shifting culture. He is too big a God for religion. It seems every generation suggests that the next generation has fallen so far away from Grace that they cannot be saved. This idea really makes God a little God, a generational God. Long after we are gone God will still be around, saving people. The same God who saved our great grandparents, our grandparents, our parents, the same God who saved us, will be here saving our children and their children. If we as Christian evangelists start believing that it is the inevitable lostness of a wicked and perverse generation that is the reason why we are not catching fish, we run the risk of being satisfied not catching fish. I used to hate to go fishing with my grandmother because she would find a shaded-area under a tree down at the creek and she would sit on that empty bucket all day and watch that stilled stopper sitting on the water and be completely at ease and satisfied. Not me! If they do not bite soon, I am ready to go! Are we sitting on our empty buckets of "traditions - the way we used to do things"? Are we OK not catching any fish? Are we satisfied sitting on the empty buckets of denominationalism, tradition and religion? Our concerns should not be how to be at ease sitting on an empty bucket but rather on what is in the bucket. Listen what David Buttrick says in his book, Speaking Parables,

"These days ministry is a peculiar vocation. Ministers and priests are more parochial than they once were. They serve their parishes but often without a wider concern for the world God loves. Too easily they can be devoted to institutional management or, worse, institutional preservation. They become program people. If they do not thrive on institution management, ministers can focus on the needs of the people they will comfort, counsel, and busy themselves with the growth and well-being of the individuals under their care. What we do not see much of these days are ministers who are first and foremost devoted to preaching and teaching and reaching out with the Word of God. Nowadays therapy and management consume the clergy."[6]

While we comfortably sit on the "empty buckets" of a self-serving institution we are losing our power to do real evangelism. We are truly getting weaker from "empty bucket" sickness. That bucket has become so comfortable to sit on that we are not encouraged to move. Under that shaded tree, sitting on that bucket, grandmother may have just been too comfortable, too tired or perhaps too lazy to move down where the creek turned where the water ran deep. Where the creek turned and the water ran deep may not have had a shaded area to sit in. The heat from the beaming sun may have made fishing in that area too uncomfortable. It might have been a day to get away from her duties and work at home. "If I catch fish, that will be fine, if I do not, well, that is alright too." These are not the words of a true fisherman. "If I catch fish, it will be great! If I do not, I want to know why, so I can determine what I need to do differently the next time". This is the thinking of a real fisherman.

There are those who would go fishing every day. Like Grandma, they do not check the fish forecast, or the lunar report or the almanac or any other scientific data to see if the fish may be biting. They do not pay any attention to the old-folk signs, like cows laying down or winds blowing out of the east. They go because they just love to go fishing. The danger in this is losing the discontentment of not catching any. "I just love to go fishing," they say. I never love going fishing. I do not love the time-consuming, resource-consuming effort it takes to "go fishing." I only do it because in order for me to catch fish, I have to go. I often think of having a house that sits right on the lake with a board-walk that leads from my back door to a deep, water hole with plenty of fish in it. I do not love to go fishing, I love catching fish. I do not love sitting there, exposing myself to the elements of the weather. I do not love being bitten by mosquitoes. I do not love going fishing. I love catching fish. When my efforts do not produce any fish, I am greatly disappointed. It is the same feeling I get when my team loses or when I miss a trophy buck. I know that I am not going to catch fish every time I go but I do not come away with being satisfied with just going. Have we lost our sense of disappointment or our feeling of "wasted time" when our evangelistic efforts do not result in catching sinners? Have we traded the passion for catching fish for the love of going fishing? Has the traditional church traded its passion for real evangelism for the love of "having church?" Every time I hear that phrase (having church) I wonder if this is what our Mission has become.

Chapter 3

ALL FISH DO NOT EAT THE SAME BAIT

WHEN I GO FISHING, IN my tackle box are about two hundred dollars' worth of fish lures and accessories. Lures of all shapes and sizes are in my box. Some made like insects, small reptiles and flies. These are the artificial ones. Then there are the live ones. There are the crickets, worms, cut-bait, shiners, etc. The reason why all these baits make up the total arsenal of a fisherman tackle box is because "all fish do not bite the same bait." There have been times when I have gone fishing with a certain bait to catch a certain kind of fish. But the fish that I went looking for were not there. However, there were other fish down there and when I discovered that the fish that I had gone looking for were not there, I changed bait and still caught fish. If our evangelistic fishing is limited to a certain species of fish, our evangelistic success will be at a minimum. In our presentation of the Gospel of Jesus Christ to a world that has so many deep-water issues, in order to reach the masses, men of every birth, the evangelistic fisherman must be familiar with the culture, habits, appetite, and thinking of all the fish in the lake. The tackle-box must have a diversity of approaches to go after all the fish in the lake. When our teaching, preaching and witnessing methods appeal to only a certain kind of fish in the lake (ethnic, age, gender, class, etc.), we are not ready to launch out into the deep.

In the last two or three decades, our society has crossed many lines that once separated people. Integration within the last decade has even made its way into the church. In our culture, class was also a factor in the separation of people. Historically the upper class would make their way to the city churches that were led by the more educated ministers. Typically, these ministers were bi-vocational who had professional secular degrees such as educators and businessmen. Their worship services were a bit stoic with a ceremonial overtone. The lower-class would feel more comfortable in the small rural settings where they did not have to show so much poise and sophistication. They could "allow the Spirit to have His way." A church that uses the proper methods of deep-water evangelism today will have a diversity of people that includes three and four generations, multiple races, gender balanced-memberships and yes, people of different sexual orientations. The first phase of getting a fish into the frying pan is to catch the fish. I do not look to see if the fish is male or female, scared or unmarked. I cannot tell how old a fish is. And to be honest I really do not care about the fish's sexual preference. I suppose there are gay fish. I put them all in the cooler or the well because come cleaning time everything that makes the fish gay will be gutted out. Once I catch them then I will clean them. We will address the fish cleaning in another chapter. I am a fundamentalist by birth and by culture and you can be sure that I have my fundamental views about the counter cultural views that are invading my fundamental turf. At the same time, I am an agent of God and while God hates sin He loves all of His creatures, unconditionally. It is my duty to share that love with all people and to press upon them that His love is unconditional. This is deep water fishing.

Chapter 4

THE FISH FINDER

WHEN I FIRST BOUGHT MY boat I wanted to equip it with all the tools that are necessary to make fishing comfortable and easy. I rigged it for night fishing, adding wiring for electricity distribution throughout the boat. I installed lights for night-fishing and placed two generators on the boat, one with a gas engine and the other powered by lithium batteries. I added a gas grill and microwave oven to prepare hot food for extended time on the water.

The most important tool that I thought I needed was a combination Fish and Depth Finder. This little instrument will not only tell me how deep the water is but it will tell me where the fish are hanging out. There are places down there in the deep, near stumps and rocks, where the deep-water drop-offs are, where the fish hang out. With this Fish and Depth Finder I will not have to guess where the fish are or how deep the water is. This is some neat little gadget. Technology has even made it easy to fish. I had an old friend of mine who thought that all of that stuff takes the joy out of fishing. The only thing that takes the joy out of fishing for me is when they are not biting; when I cannot get on top of them.

Technology has also made it easy for the Church to locate the deep water and the places where the un-saved hangs out. The age of technology has overwhelmed us with gadgets that literally control our every move. I often think about a wish I wished I had. I wish that I could magically bring my granddaddy back to life today from where he left off when he died in the fifties. This thought gives me an exciting, amazing but frightening feeling. Truly this would be a mighty culture shock to my granddaddy, to say the least. In fact granddaddy would probably think that he was in another world. He would see things that he never would have dreamed of, even in his wildest imagination. No doubt he had already been shocked by the telephone, airplane, automobile and television in his life time. But if he had lived on another sixty years he would have witnessed the greatest advancement in innovations since civilization begin. Rapid advance in computer technology, telephony, biotechnology, nanotechnology, many other scientific advancements have redefined our world and the way we live to a degree that granddaddy perhaps could not survive the adjustment.

However, one thing my granddaddy would recognize and be comfortable in is his membership church. It still sits in the same place, although isolated. They are still singing the same songs. The service time and day are still the same. The preacher is still communicating the gospel the same way. The feast days are still the same. The special day programs are still the same. The method of collecting offerings is still the same. The world that we live in, operates and do business in, work, play and socialize in, has advanced far beyond the reach of the traditional church. Rather than finding ways to "serve the present age," many church leaders condemn those who look for new and innovative ways to evangelize.

I heard of a church that had their worship services on Friday and late Saturday night. When I shared this with a fellow minister friend of mine, they thought that this was theologically inappropriate. "Sunday is the day to go to church. It is the first day of the week, the observance of the Lord's Resurrection," he said. The reasoning for having theses service at these times had to do with the number of people who were members of the church who worked in the afternoons and on Sundays.

Technology

In some churches, technology is seen as satanic and should not be allowed in the worship place. Sure, use computers to keep your records and maintain your accounting but they should not be allowed in the sanctuary. The truth is, the Church cannot navigate, and it cannot locate the fish unless it uses technology. Technology is where the fish are. Technology is the church's connection to the deep waters of a sinful world. If the church is to be successful in deep water fishing, it must retool itself with the technology needed to locate and navigate the deep water and find the fish. For example, most of us rarely carry cash money. When we do financial transactions, we either use our credit card, debit card of some smart-phone apps. The giving options in today's church environment should not be limited to just dropping cash or check in a basket. Every church should have a debit card machine for givers to use their debit cards when bringing their tithes and offerings. There are apps for smart phones user that only takes thirty seconds to make a contribution, without getting out of your seat.

About three years ago I got a call from a member who worked on a cruise liner. She asked if there was a way she could tithe without having to mail it. After some research, I found an App that could be downloaded on the smartphone. We instituted an App for giving and the member were able to give in thirty seconds on her smart phone.

Some members of our church pay their tithes and offering with "electronic bill pay." Others just have monthly transfers from their bank account to the church's bank account. Just the other day while I was in Memphis Tennessee, I saw a friend who I had loaned some money some time before. He wrote a check and I used my smartphone, took a picture with the camera, and deposited the money in my bank account. I did not have to wait until I returned home to go to the bank. In an age of electronic economics, it would be wise for the church to move to the deep waters of electronic financing.

Social Media

Forty years ago, I remember when we needed to get the word out about a special occasion such as a revival or gospel singing or some other non-regular scheduled event, we would place advertisements in the local newspaper, send public service announcements to the local radio stations and/or send announcements by mail or courier to sister churches. In this environment of technology none of these things are necessary. The surest and most exhaustive way to spread the word is through social media. If a church would engage its members in a concentrated effort to send information to the masses it has to do nothing more than turn to Facebook.

According to a research done by the Pew Research Center - Internet, Science & Technology, as of January 2014, 74% of online adults use social networking sites.

Facebook friend counts

Median # of friends by age

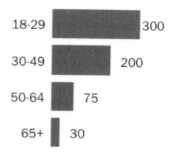

Pew Research Center's Internet Project survey, August 7-September 16, 2013.

PEW RESEARCH CENTER

- 39% of adult Facebook users have between 1 and 100 Facebook friends
- 23% have 101-250 friends
- 20% have 251-500 friends
- 15% have more than 500 friends

Among adult Facebook users, the average number of friends is 338, and the median (midpoint) number of friends is 200. In other words, half of all Facebook users have more than 200 friends, and half have less than 200.

Younger users tend to have significantly larger friend networks than older users: 27% of 18-29 year old Facebook users have more than 500 friends in their network, while 72% of users age 65+ have 100 friends or fewer.[7]

If the evangelistic work of the Church would use this incredible media to spread the gospel to the lost, not focusing on getting unbelievers to "come to my church" but "Come unto Him all ye that are weighted down with the cares and troubles of this life to find rest," the church could begin fishing in the deep waters of technological innovations. A lot more people can be evangelized through Facebook than can be reached by going from door to door. With the statistics that show the large numbers of friends, not strangers, every believer can make evangelism a personal commitment and, one-on-one, lead the unsaved to Christ. A "Facebook Church" could be a powerful tool for evangelizing the lost.

There is a member of the ministerial staff at our church who carries on a great personal ministry through Facebook. The number of friends that engage in his ministry is vast. He uses video clips of music, preaching, worship and praise. He shares proverbs and inspirational saying that are revealed to him as well as those he hears from other. The interactions of friends in conversations and testimonies are incredible. All this takes place weekly on Facebook.

Technology is here to stay and it can benefit the Church when it navigates deep water.

Technology not only tells us how deep the water is and where the fish are located, it also tells us where we are.

I thought I had all the technology I needed until one day my brother and I decided to go to Lake Talquin at Quincy Florida. I had gone before with some friends and the crappies from that lake were bigger than I had ever seen before. So, he and I went there one day and we located the deep water with our depth finder and the deep water with our fish finder. And we filled our coolers. When we were ready to come back to the docks late that night, we had lost our sense of direction and did not know where we were. It is a scary feeling to be out on a big unfamiliar lake at night and not know where you are. After a long time of searching, we finally found the docks. However, I swore that would never happen to me again. I knew I had one more piece of technology to buy and that was a GPS for the lakes. I immediately had one installed on my boat. I installed that GPS on my boat because I learned pretty quickly, it is not only necessary to know where the deep water is and where the fish are, the fisherman needs to know where he/she is.

"Let them alone. They are blind leaders of the blind. And if the blind leads the blind, both will fall into a ditch." (Matt 15:14)

Have we gotten lost along "the way?" Listen to what Christ wrote to the Church at Ephesus about where they had come to.

> *Nevertheless, I have this against you, that you have left your first love.* [5] *Remember therefore from where you have fallen; repent and do the first works, or else I will come to you quickly and remove your lampstand from its place—unless you repent. (Rev 2:4-5)*

Has Jesus, himself walked away from our evangelism. When I started to preach, I remember the late Rev. R.B. Smith Jr. doing an exegete on Matthew 28:19-20KJV, "*Go ye therefore, and teach all nations, baptizing them in the name of the Father, and of the Son, and of the Holy Ghost: Teaching them to observe all things whatsoever I have commanded you: and, lo, I am with you **alway**, even unto the end of the world. Amen.*" Rev. Smith would always emphasize that the word *alway* was not the same as always. At first I just thought that he was just playing on words. He was misinterpreting old-English with modern day English. Then he said, "What Jesus was saying to His preachers 'I will be with you All The Way.' Not all the ways. All 'The Way.' As long as you stay with 'The Way,' I will be with you. But when you leave 'The Way,' I will no longer be with you." Whether this is incorrect exegesis or not it is another debate. But we can all understand

Rev. Smith's contention. It seems to be correct theology. When Christ is no longer with us in our faith, in our preaching and in our anointing, our evangelistic fishing license is essentially revoked and we forfeit the power that we need to successfully fish in deep waters.

The Church at Ephesus was at risk of losing its divine accreditation and becoming just an organization that was nothing more than a social club. They were at risk because they had "left their first love." What was that first love? Some said that *"the first love which characterized the Ephesians was the zeal and ardor with which they embraced their salvation as they realized they loved Christ because He first loved them."* Matthew Henry, in his Concise Commentary says *"The sin Christ charged this church with, is, not the having left and forsaken the object of love, but having lost the fervent degree of it that at first appeared. Christ is displeased with his people, when he sees them grow remiss and cold toward him. Surely this mention in Scripture, of Christians forsaking their first love, reproves those who speak of it with carelessness, and thus try to excuse indifference and sloth in themselves and others; our Saviour considers this indifference as sinful. They must repent: they must be grieved and ashamed for their sinful declining, and humbly confess it in the sight of God.*[8]

We can simplify this answer by simply saying "Jesus." They had left Jesus—the Gospel Message. The preachers of old who mentored me conveyed to me what was conveyed to them by their mentors and that is "No sermon is ever complete, no preacher's job is ever done, nothing truthful can be declared until you have declared the Gospel of Jesus Christ – The Good News – The Death, Burial and Resurrection of Jesus Christ. They echoed the sentiment of the gospel preacher, "apart from Jesus Christ, the preacher has nothing to say." The Apostle Paul wrote to the Church at Corinth when they were evaluating his preaching legitimacy, *"And I, brethren, when I came to you, I did not come with excellence of speech or of wisdom declaring to you the testimony of God. For I determined not to know anything among you except Jesus Christ and Him crucified." (1 Corin 2:1-2)* It was the preaching of Jesus Christ that perpetuated the New Testament Church. And it was done in the face of great hostilities and persecutions.

It is amazing that the charter members of the New Testament church were only one hundred and twenty in number (Acts 1:15). Their primary message was the offering of abundant life from one who had lost His' on a crucified cross. Yet when we read Acts 2:41, 2:47, 4:4, we can figure that from chapter 1 to chapter 6, the church had grown from one hundred and twenty members to over 10,000. They had but only one message (bait), "Jesus Christ and Him crucified." Their preaching was rooted in Old Testament scripture and their knowledge of the crucified Christ. With this, they "turned the world upside down" (Acts 17:6). The success was not in the excellence of their speech, they were seen as ignorant and unlearned (Acts 4:13). They had only the message of the gospel, "Christ and Him Crucified."

The feeders for the New Testament Church were not the homes and communities of Christian people. The newly converts were not descendants of Christ-believers. For the most part they were from the communities that initially rejected the gospel message. When the evangelists went fishing, they had to go to the deep waters of rejection and persecution, where the fish were.

Successful deep-water fishing will only take place when the messenger of God commits to the God-glorifying, Christ-centered, Spirit-empowered preaching. It does not matter if the sermon text is taken from Genesis, Exodus, Numbers, Leviticus, Deuteronomy or the Old Testament history books or the poetic books or the prophetic books, the subject must be about Jesus Christ. As Steven Lawson so eloquently stated in his book, The Kind of Preaching God Blesses, *"The kind of preaching God blesses, specifically the proclamation that exalts the crucified Christ by the power of the Spirit."* Lawson further states that "In this present hour, preaching that is devoid of the person and work of Christ is all too often commonplace. Such lifeless words are a snare into which many pulpits have fallen, the deadly trap in which the Lord Jesus is minimized, if not all together absent. Rather than giving

Him the central place of preeminence, Jesus is demoted to the periphery. Instead of being in the spotlight, Christ is left standing in the shadows."[10] I am reminded of the Church at Laodicea (Rev 3:20) where Jesus stood outside of the door knocking to get in. They were proclaiming that they were a great church, rich and had no need of anything, yet Jesus was missing. No doubt they were singing the songs dedicated to his name, baptizing those who confessed their faith in Him and claiming to be His agents, but He was locked out. He was locked out because He had to knock to get in. The great tragedy in the Christian Church today is that the Gospel of Jesus Christ is being displaced by a watered-down gospel that cannot inspire the believers, let-a-lone hardened sinners. To be successful at deep water evangelism, the supreme majesty of Christ Himself must be expounded in our preaching consistently.

Have we become like the Pharisees when Jesus said to them;

> *"You search the Scriptures, for in them you think you have eternal life; and these are they which testify of Me?" (John 5:39)*

Have we left the only true power in evangelism for some motivational inspiration that sounds good but is soon forgotten? Is our tackle-box missing the very thing that guarantees us that we will be successful in deep waters? Have we come to believe that much of the Bible has become outdated and disconnected with humanity? Our tackle-box is the Bible and it is complete with everything we need to catch fish in deep waters, no matter what kind of fish we go after.

> *Then I said, 'Behold, I have come— In the volume of the book it is written of Me— To do Your will, O God.' (Heb 10:7)*

The optimum word in this verse is "volume," the whole book. At the climactic closing of the old preachers' sermons, they would always end in a celebratory focus on the death, burial and resurrection of Jesus Christ. No matter what book they preached from. Shift to the deep waters of our religion today and it is not unusual to hear a sermon preached that Jesus Christ's name is not even mentioned. The deep-water fisherman can become biblically lost in doctrine, in principles, in biblical interpretation and application if Jesus is not our Global Positioning System (GPS). Before we find the deep water, before we find the fish, we need to know Jesus, more specifically, know His Call on our lives and His purpose for dying. The waves of change are too strong in the deep. It is too dangerous out there to be caught without the "life jacket." It's too dangerous to be out there in a boat in the deep, windy, waters without the right anchor. It can get pretty scary in the dark when you do not know where you are. We could easily be swept away into the unknown darkness and have trouble getting back to the dock. We could easily get so involved in catching fish that we lose our sense of direction. Get yourself the GPS so you will always know where you are.

Chapter 5

DEEP-WATER COURAGE

"HOW DEEP IS THIS WATER," she asked. I looked at the depth finder. "Forty two feet," I responded. "Forty-two Feet?!!!" Yes, forty-two feet, at night, with the boat rocking in the wind. Can you really enjoy fishing in that kind of situation? Is catching fish really that important? Can you really focus on fishing in forty- two feet of water on a windy, dark night, in a small boat? That takes some courage. Well, the truth is this is the description, in a metaphorical way, of the godless society that we live in and the rising demands it has placed upon the Church to adjust to its cultural mandates. Out there on the open lake of a godless society, where the issues are deep and the winds of adversity blow strongly, it takes courage to stay the course. If there is one thing the evangelistic fisherman must have it is courage. Courage to confront the adversary, courage to stand on the Word of God with boldness and courage to face criticism, ridicule and even persecution.

Reflecting on the beginning of the early church, in that upper room, there was just a small number of uneducated converts who were the charter members. They were not doctors of theology, or well versed and experienced leaders. Most were just working-class people. On top of that, the message they had was a message of salvation by one who lost His life. In a very hostile world, they used this, the Gospel of one who claimed to be able to save others but unable to save himself and turned the world upside down (Acts 17:6). We can see that from this gathering (Act 1:15) to chapter 6, the Church had grown to more than ten thousand. How did this happen? Passion, Power and Courage.

The early church did not grow from outreach programs, trained doctors, hermeneutical experts, exegetical orators. It grew out of suffering. Tertullian the Great, the father of Latin Christianity and the founder of Western theology, in his treatise defending Christianity said, "The Blood of the Martyrs is the Seed of the Church."[11]

> *(Acts 8:1) At that time a great persecution arose against the church which was at Jerusalem; and they were all scattered throughout the regions of Judea and Samaria,*

> *(Acts 8:4) Therefore those who were scattered went everywhere preaching the word.*

Since the establishment of the papacy, the New Testament has had to deal with the politics of religion – church politics. And even while Jesus was here there was a sniff of politics among His disciples who were campaigning for position in their ranks. In our democratic congregations and board-controlled churches, the preacher is always under the scrutinizing eyes of those who have the power to take his/her job away from him/her. There is always that awareness of offending the masses or going against what the people want. There is always that danger of offending a powerful board member, of insulting an elderly lady or standing against unchristian activities. There is the danger of rejecting the godlessness of a sinful world that demands that the Church embrace it.

Paul reminded Timothy it would happen and admonished him to have courage;

For the time will come when they will not endure sound doctrine, but according to their own desires, because they have itching ears, they will heap up for themselves teachers; 4 and they will turn their ears away from the truth, and be turned aside to fables. 5 But you be watchful in all things, endure afflictions, do the work of an evangelist, fulfill your ministry. (2 Tim 4:3-5)

The deep-water evangelist must come to grips with his/her fears. The fear of being fired, rejected and attacked. There are too many of us who are intimidated by the ungodliness of the world, too many who are too ready to embrace the liberal and ungodly mandates of an ungodly world. Too many who are afraid they will be replaced with those who are willing to give the people what they want rather than what they need.

How does the evangelistic fisherman fish in this fear? The courage we have is always in proportion to our faith in God. Jesus said to His disciples, "Be mindful, I am sending you out as you were sheep in the midst of wolves." The only way that a sheep can ever feel courageous and confident in the vicinity of wolves is because of the presence of the shepherd. If our courage is fueled by our confidence in our own power and ability, we will soon discover how truly weak we are. Our weakness must always be in His strength.

Our confidence and courage grows as we become more knowledgeable about navigating and fishing in the deep. The days of bought, canned sermons are over. There were times when the preacher could go to a convention, buy 104 sermons (two sermons per Sunday) and a few special-day sermons and did not have to pick up the bible for a whole year. However, canned sermons do not inspire biblical exploration. The deep-water evangelist must become, not only familiar with the book, but a "rightly divider of the Word of Truth." Consistent study and meditation are essential to going to the deep. Expanding our understanding of the scriptures and applications through the prisms of current events and the times that we live in are absolutely necessary in order to be safe in deep water evangelism. The reason why many preachers have fears of going to the deep is because they know they are not anchored enough in the Word. The true deep-water evangelist must expand in his knowledge base, not only of the Word of God but in the society he/she lives in, and the people who are the objects and subjects of his/her evangelistic efforts. To do this, one must become an avid reader; a student of not just theology but psychology, sociology, biology, technology, physiology and as many other "ologies" as possible.

Chapter 6

FISH CLEANING

MY FREEZER IS ALWAYS FILLED with fish. Why? Because most of the friends who go fishing with me love to catch fish but they do not like cleaning them. And so after a good day of fishing when we return home late, they just do not want to clean fish. So they say to me, "You can have them." Usually it is late night when we come home and so I will stop at a curb store and buy a couple of bags of ice and pour into the cooler on top of the fish to keep until morning. On the back side of my yard, I have built a home-made fish-cleaning station. First thing in the morning I go through the pain-staking effort to clean the fish, bag them and put them in the freezer. The real truth is, if you are going to be a fisherman, you have got to come to grips with the responsibility of cleaning them. I know a place I can take my fish to have them cleaned and occasionally I do. But for the most part, I clean my own fish and the fish that others caught but do not want to clean. Yes, I clean them too. And so, my freezer is filled with fish.

When we catch fish, evangelistically, and defer in cleaning them, we essentially say to religion, "you can have them." Religion makes them ready to use for its own purpose. It prepares them for its own consumption and freezes them for keeps. My sisters and others often call and ask if I have any fish in the freezer. I always say, "I have plenty. Come on over and get some". And so, I provide fish for whoever wants some. The same happens when religion freezes fish that the fishermen neglected to clean. It is a provisioning resource for the local churches. The fish moved to the place where it seemed to be wanted. Religion has plenty of un-cleaned fish, ready to disperse to any local church. And so it is not unusual for fish to move from house to house. Religion is the feeder for the local church, not unsaved sinners. Most of the fish in the local church are fish that the fishermen who caught them did not take the time to clean them. There seems to be more work and more joy in getting the ninety and nine than over the one (Luke 15:7). The consequential tragedy is that far too many of the fish that have been caught have not been properly cleaned or properly conditioned for "the work of the ministry." This is mainly because, for many evangelistic fishermen, evangelistic fishing has been a sport. Fishermen who catch fish and throw them back or give them away only fish for sport or for amusement. And then there are many fishermen who go fishing and come home with no one wanting to take the fish they will freeze them without cleaning them with the intention of giving them away at a later time, as they are. Some even say, it is better to freeze the fish and clean them when they are ready to cook. I have never tried it. It just seems to me, as a fisherman, the best time to clean the fish is after you catch them. As evangelistic fishermen, we have allowed so many of the fish to freeze in religion that many of our churches are not equipped and prepared for the "Great Commission." Sure, we can "have church," put on our Sunday Morning worship show. But making disciples that are ready for the "Great Commission," to a great degree, the evangelistic fishermen have failed. And so, the church has lost its love and passion for witnessing and evangelizing.

We have not prepared the fish for Kingdom consumption through training and development. Our sermons discourses have been entertaining, amusing at best. Our teaching has veered away from Christ and the Power of the Holy Spirit and our work has been focused on our own benefit rather than the benefit of the unsaved. As he did with the Church at Ephesus (Rev 2:4), Pergamos (Rev 2:14) and Thyatira (Rev 2:20), Jesus has "somewhat against us." We have left the Church's first love.

The evangelistic fisherman must come to know that catching fish does not make you a true fisherman. A true evangelistic fisherman must know that the real work begins after the fish have been caught. The real work is in the cleaning.

And so it does not matter what the fish has in its guts or what kind of fish get caught on the hook or in the net, they all need cleaning. They all come not ready for use…ALL.

The lakes that we fish from are all dirty. Beyond the debris and chemicals that are dumped in by man, just the waste from the life in the lake is cause to be aware that everything that comes from the lake needs cleaning. Some people do not eat catfish. They say they are scavengers. They all are. Have you ever noticed that you never see a sick or dead fish on the lake? Have you ever noticed that you do not see dead animals floating in the lake? You have got to know that fish get sick and die. You have got to know that other animals drown. Where do they go? I assure you that they are not all eaten by catfish. You say catfish are bottom feeders. Some of my best bream fishing is with worms on the bottom. What am I saying? They are all scavengers. There are no clean fish.

You cannot eat the fish you caught before you clean them. The same goes for the Kingdom. They are of no use to the kingdom until they have gone through a cleaning cycle.

In many ways we have abandoned evangelistic preaching and teaching and have traded it off for a watered down gospel that places no demand on Christian living.

It seems that the church has become satisfied orientating new converts to religion rather than developing them in Christ. In Dietrich Bonhoeffer's book, *The Cost of Discipleship,* he says,

> "If our Christianity has ceased to be serious about discipleship, if we have watered down the gospel into emotional uplift which makes no costly demands and which fails to distinguish between natural and Christian existence, then we cannot help regarding the cross as an ordinary everyday calamity, as one of the trials of life[12]

We seem to spend most of our preaching and teaching time talking about how "We" can overcome the world's problem rather than submitting ourselves to Christ to be delivered. The reality is that we cannot clean ourselves, only Christ can. The Word and the Spirit are the only agents that can truly bring cleansing to the fish. Our evangelism must return to its first love. Those first evangelists after the Resurrection had but only one central message, "Jesus Christ and Him Crucified."

Chapter 7

The Church and Ethnic Diversity

In a question-and-answer session after a lecture on race at Western Michigan University in 1963, Martin Luther King, Jr. said, "Christians in the United States fail to live out the tenets of their faith." "We must face the fact that in America the church is still the most segregated major institution in America. At 11:00 on Sunday morning when we stand and sing and Christ has no east or west, we stand at the most segregated hour in this nation. This is tragic."

How did this come to be? In an article from the African American Registry entitled "*The Black Church*," A Brief History, we read

> **Post -Civil War:** After emancipation, black churches became virtually the only place for African-Americans to find refuge. Blacks moved away from the "brush-harbors" that they retreated

to for solace as slaves. Formally during this time a church separation petition was filed by thirty-eight black members of the predominantly white Fairfield Baptist Church in Northumberland County, Virginia, in 1867. Referring to the new political and social status of African Americans, the petitioners said they wanted to "place ourselves where we could best promote our mutual good" and suggested "a separate church organization as the best possible way. A month later the white members of the church unanimously acceded to the petitioners' request, setting the stage for the creation of the all-black Shiloh Baptist Church.

Once established, Black Churches spread rapidly throughout the South; the Baptist churches led in this proliferation. The 1800's ushered in many milestones that built on the foundation of the Black Church. To mention just a few, 1808 celebrated the founding of Abyssinian Baptist Church in New York City. Black Americans along with a group of Ethiopian merchants were unwilling to accept racially segregated seating of the First Baptist Church of New York City. They withdrew forever their membership and established themselves in a building on Anthony Street (later Worth Street) calling it the Abyssinian

Baptist Church. The name was inspired by the nation from which the merchants of Ethiopia had come, Abyssinia[13]

Because of the historical racial divide in America, the universal intent of the Church, mandated by Jesus Christ in the Great Commission that embraces "all nations" was relegated to people who look like us. The Church came to be identified as "The White Church" and "The Black Church." In the Afro American church, particularly before and during the period of civil rights, the church was not only the place for religious assembly, but it was the hub of social relations and strategic operations for the Black Community.

In that same article from the African American Registry entitled "*The Black Church*," A Brief History, we read,

Nineteenth-century black churches ministered to the needs of the soul and served a host of secular functions, which placed them squarely in the center of black social life. Church buildings doubled as community meeting centers and schools until permanent structures could be built, and during Reconstruction they served as political halls. The black church provided shelter for visitors as well as temporary community theaters and concert halls where religious and secular plays and programs were presented.

In a blurring of spiritual and social functions church members provided care for the sick or incapacitated and financial assistance to students bound for college. They also sponsored virtually all the many fraternal lodges that emerged in the nineteenth-century South. As racially motivated violence and terrorism ran rampant across the country, Black churches were staunch in their resistance. [14]

During the Movement, the Church was the training grounds and the place where information related to the community and the struggle was disseminated to the community. The leadership that was needed to strategize and lead a successful movement was done mostly by the black preacher. The gospel was preached from a social justice-injustice perspective. Using the story of Israel as a metaphor, the Black Church ushered the Black Community through the perilous period of the Civil Rights Movement. During that time the White Church was mostly silent and, to a great degree, its members were complicit in the discriminatory practices that the Black Church was fighting against. The ministries of the two churches were culturally different. The religion of those with the quest for freedom was experientially different from those who had never been enslaved. Both churches would use the Gospel as a support to legitimize their social and ethnic theology. Their songs were different. Their prayers were different. Their preaching, style and content, all were different. Subsequently the Church was divided along racial lines.

After the Civil Right Era that ushered in integration and social diversity along with the mass immigration of foreigners to the US, the society that we live in today is remarkably different than it was forty years ago. Cross-cultural, cross-ethnicity and diverse work, social and public places have challenged the church to rethink how it serves the gospel to those who are saved and how it offers it to those who are lost.

The reality is that the fish of ethnic diversity have moved in every place but the church. While some churches have made efforts to racially diversify their congregations, the most segregated time of the week is still Sunday morning.

"Today, diverse churches remain rare," said Ed Stetzer, president of LifeWay Research, "partly because of human nature". "Everybody wants diversity," said Stetzer. "But many don't want to be around people who are different."[15]

While the historical black church has always been a center to provide comfort and counsel to the Afro-

American community and must continue to do so, the cultural language that was used to inform and counsel during the times of segregation and racial conflict has to be tempered with a sensitivity that does not racially offend others. The Church of Jesus Christ is not a Black Church or a White Church or a Latino Church, it is a Christian Church.

In recent years my presentation of the Gospel has become even more sensitively aware that there is a continuously increasing number of people who sit in the pews that are a product of their genes, their environment, their culture, their generation, their intellectual exposures, their experiences and much more. The last thing they need to hear from the podium of the Gospel is a Word from a God who loves only a certain kind of people. While their enemy is the same with them all, their battles are different. When people come to hear the message of the gospel, their great need is to hear "good news" at a time when their conditions say there is none. They need to hear that the compassionate Father is not a respecter of persons when he show forth his love.

> *(Gal 3:26-29)*
> *For you are all sons of God through faith in Christ Jesus. For as many of you as were baptized into Christ have put on Christ. There is neither Jew nor Greek, there is neither slave nor free, there is neither male*

*nor female; for you are all one in Christ Jesus. And
if you are Christ's, then you are Abraham's seed, and
heirs according to the promise.*

*(Rom 2:11)
For there is no partiality with God*

We know that we have a long ways to go in race
relations and the great need for God's love in humanity.
We have so much of the past to overcome. The truth is that
many of us who experienced so much hatred, oppression
and exploitation during those years may never be able
to completely overcome such dreadful experiences.
However, the Church can lead the way. Perhaps, the
reason why racial harmony has not advanced in our
society, in spite of the advancement in social diversity, is
because the Church has not led the way.

It is deep water leadership. It requires us to wade out
into the deep waters of the healing ministry of Christ,
reaching far beyond "ethnic theology." It demands that
we leave behind the shallowness of bigotry and hatred,
and the shallowness of only being able to preach and
teach a people who only look like us or only fit into
the frame-work of my ethnicity. The churches that
will survive and advance in the 21st century will be the
churches that move to the deep waters of diversity to
minister to all races and all cultures. The gospel, the

application, and the interpretation of the Word of God must be color blind, racially and culturally sensitive and minister to a diversified people. This requires a deeper study in the Word of God, a passion for all people and an intimate knowledge of who God is. It calls on us to rethink our biblical interpretations and applications. It demands that we retool our theology for deep-water evangelism.

Denominational Organization

For most of us, it is not uncommon to find ourselves in conversations about the assessment of our denominational organizations. Associations, Union Meetings, regional, state and national organizations, all are in free-fall. Churches are walking away. I was at the national convention in September and while the number of the convention goers seemed to remain the same it was noticeable that the number of registration badges pinned on their lapels were very few. They are still using church funds to go to the convention but it is not for denominational business, it is an annual vacation. When asked, "Why have you lost interest in the denomination's work," the reply always seems to be, "I see no benefits that the organization offers to the local church". They go on to say, "The churches that are making a difference in the evangelistic growth of the Church do not look to our denominational organizations for leadership, primarily because they have not shifted to deep-water evangelism."

I want to quote again what I quoted earlier in chapter 2, what David Buttrick says in his book, *Speaking Parables*,

> "These days ministry is a peculiar vocation. Ministers and priests are more parochial than they once were. They serve their parishes but often without a wider concern for the world God loves. Too easily they can be devoted to institutional management or, worse, institutional preservation. They become program people. If they do not thrive on institution management, ministers can focus on the needs of the people, they will comfort, counsel, and busy themselves with the growth and well-being of the individuals under their care. What we do not see much of these days are ministers who are first and foremost devoted to preaching and teaching and reaching out with the Word of God. Nowadays therapy and management consume the clergy."[16]

Is this true? Are we more concerned about the polity and politics of our denomination than we are over the immoral conduct of our members? Is our denomination more important than the lost sinner? The great conflict between Jesus Christ and the Jews was about "the institution."

John 11:49-15

And one of them, Caiaphas, being high priest that year, said to them, "You know nothing at all, nor do you consider that it is expedient for us that one man should die for the people, and not that the whole nation should perish."

This "nation" that Caiaphas is talking about is their religious institution.

They were so intent on preserving the institution that they missed the greatest opportunity of humanity; Jesus.

I am not advocating getting rid of the institutional organizations that have given structure and support to the local church. But I am advocating the retooling of them for deep-water fishing; for relevance.

The key to doing this is to create a culture of local-church services, a Christ-like ministry that does not invest its time in the preservation of the institution and those who are determined to preserve the high positions but dedicated to providing services and support to the local churches. Particularly those small churches that are adversely affected by the "fish have moved" reality.

The truth is I never hear from the Convention unless there is a request for funds. The need to keep the institution funded is not a concern for those who are struggling to keep their own heads above financial waters. If the

Convention would access the problems of the regional and local churches and provide leadership in ministry assessments, demographics effects, consolidations, combining resources, partnerships, etc., this might serve to secure the support base. On line training for pastors and leaders who have deficiencies in their roles, negotiating with companies that sells products, i.e. audio-video equipment, furniture, computers, etc. for significant discounts are just a few of the things the Convention can do for the constituent churches.

Associations

Associations were, in part, established to give the autonomous churches a means to be connected to the denominational order as well as provide common structure and disciplines. Fifty years ago most of the Baptist churches were a member of an Association. Today, most are not. The number of churches that are cutting ties with associations are rapidly increasing. When asked, "Why did you withdraw your membership?" The reply seems always to be, "there are no benefits for the church."

Associations can still be a great tool for the work of the Church. However, there is a need for them to retool and launch out into deeper waters; using the long-time fellowships that were an integral part of the association and form new partnerships.

Chapter 8

FELLOWSHIP VS PARTNERSHIP

[6] And when they had this done, they enclosed a great multitude of fishes: and their net brake. [7] And they beckoned unto their partners, which were in the other ship, that they should come and help them. And they came, and filled both the ships, so that they began to sink.

SINCE THE BEGINNING OF THE congregational church, when each group of members were autonomous of the others, there have been the activities of "fellowship." During the early days of the Afro-American church, particularly the rural churches who only had assembly once a month, a continuous fellowship was carried on among the churches in a specific region that brought congregations together. This fellowship not only brought the congregations together at one time, it also provided means for members of one congregation to worship with other congregations on those Sundays when there were no assemblies at the home church. Over the years this became important to the churches because it helped fill the pews and, beyond that, put more money in the basket. After a while this became a means of fundraising. The Fish have Moved! Perhaps the time has come when there needs to be some deep-water thinking on reasons and purposes congregations are brought together. Given the great undertaking of "Deep Water Fishing" and the power, courage and resources needed to be successful, it may be time that we shift from "shallow water" fellowship to "deep water" partnership. In the text, both ships are filled because someone saw the need for partnership. Notice, in verse seven, their association was a partnership-association, not a fellowship-association. Has autonomy led us into an age of competitiveness and turf-ism that has rendered us powerless to collaborate in partnership? Have we become a church community that our primary objective is to have church with other churches for the purpose of fundraising? Would not our time be better spent in collaborating with other congregations in partnership to serve the greater community and to evangelize the world? Would not we be more productive in evangelism if we were able to realize that there are enough fish in the deep water that will provide an ample supply of converts for all the churches? Has the time we spent in futility in the shallow waters caused us to believe that there are not enough fish in the lake for us all? There are plenty of fish in the lake, they have just moved!

If our associations, unions and church annual fellowships would consider shifting from fellowship to partnership, this could ignite a new passion to fish, because the evangelistic fishermen would be able to see how their services and contributions impact the church. When we look at a community that is in desperate need of so many things and services, we do not have to be creative to identify missions that two or more churches can join their forces and resources together for one common purpose.

About ten years ago, Pastor Daniel Simmons and I were attending an AIDS seminar in Memphis, Tennessee and I mentioned to him about creating a line item in our budget that would be for the purpose of human services beyond our congregation. He informed me of a vision that God had laid on his heart to open a clinic for the purpose of providing health care for those who could not maintain health insurance or afford needed health care. At that time his vision had not taken much form with the exception of some key people whom he had brought on board. I informed him of the financial limitations of our church but would love to become a partner in this vision. The vision did not birth in me and I had no desire to take on any ownership. After talking to our leadership team and finance folk, we were on board. We needed a place to house the clinic. Pastor Simmons and I met with the CEO of Phoebe Putney Hospital ask the hospital to partner with us for the purpose of providing the services. The CEO honored our request and agreed to provide the building (a vacant doctor's office with examination rooms) and the utilities, for one dollar a year. The hospital maintenance department had the building painted and made all necessary repairs. Through the relationship of a member of Pastor Simmons church and a widow of a doctor in his home town, this doctor's widow became aware of our needs to acquire the medical supplies and equipment for the examination rooms. She gave to the clinic, from the office of her recently departed husband, everything that was needed for the examination rooms. As the words got out, doctors from all across the community volunteered free hours and days to treat the patients. Retired nurses and office workers stepped up and volunteered their time to man the office and examination rooms. Over the years major donors have come forward and joined in partnership in this mission. There is so much more to say about this partnership and what others have done. When the other boats saw the overflowing of God's work, we had only but to beckon for them to join us. We have not mentioned all the dedicated people that have become part of the partnership in contributions and services or the number of people that the clinic has served or the many programs in health care that the clinic has provided. It is amazing to see what God will do when our missions and goals become larger than we are. It is amazing to see what God will do when partnerships are formed for the sole purpose of serving His people. Through the "partnership," I have discovered that "fellowship" is more personable and genuine.

Our community is suffering badly from the effects of some deep-water issues. Drug-abuse, crime, teen and unwed pregnancies, school drop-outs, juvenile delinquency, to name a few. These deep-water issues are devastating to the core fiber of our faith-heritage, our families and communities. Without correction, the Church will invariably become insignificant and inconsequential. Rather than folding our nets and calling it quits because we can no longer catch fish, we should consider forming partnerships and launching out into the deep waters together. There are plenty of fish out there in the deep. However, they will not be easy to catch if we go it alone. But if we join together we can once again fill all the boats.

Chapter 9

THE STRANGE FISH

IT WAS A STRANGE LOOKING fish. A walleye, a pickerel, a pike, crossed-bred with a bass? Whatever it was I had never caught one before. I was fishing this nice lake at a beautiful resort called the Resora. I had caught quite a few large-mouth bass, a few crappies and my brother had caught some breams. You know the typical fish one would expect to catch in a Georgia lake. My cooler was full. I had a packed house and with the lure I was using, they could not resist. Just when I was satisfied with today's catch, he hit it. Not much fight but his way of resistance was different. Instead of pulling and fighting and jumping, it ran horizontally across the water like lightening. What is it? When I first got a glimpse of it I thought it might be a pre-historic fish that had survived the ages. The lake is a deep-wooded, back-water- natural lake that seems to have been there since the beginning of time and I had said before, "no telling what's out there."

And so, when I saw it I had this crazy notion that he was a stranger.

I was a little reluctant to put my hands on it. I wondered if it might be poison or if it might have a form of intelligence that made it smart enough to play dead and bite off my hand when I least expected. The thing had a long mouth with plenty of sharp teeth. I finally got enough courage to touch it, for the sole purpose of getting it unhooked from my line and throwing it back to the waters. Yet, when I touched the thing, it felt familiar; tender, scaly, fishy and edible. I said to myself, "I came to fish. This is a fish" and into the cooler it went. I brought the fish home, cleaned it, cooked it and decided that I alone would eat it. Not that I did not want to share but because I still was not convinced that it should be treated like the other fish. Um Um, that was some tasty treat. I loved it. You know what? Since that day I caught the stranger, I have caught many more. I went fishing Friday and caught four. They seemed to be the only one striking. I give away quite a few fish, but I keep these for myself.

When I was a young teenager we were visiting a church one Sunday and just about the time the preacher began to preach, in walked this hoboish looking man with poor hygiene, unshaven and un-combed hair. He sat on the front pew and lit a cigarette and began to respond to every word the preacher said. The response was the typical response when the preacher would ask,

"Can I get a witness." But because he was different, because he did not meet the church's dress code or had violated etiquette by lighting a cigarette and distracting the congregation from paying attention to the preacher, two deacons quickly escorted him out of the sanctuary and demanded he should not return. After expelling him from the premises, they returned to the assembly and finished having church.

At the dinner table that Sunday afternoon our family discussed what the church leaders should have done about the stranger who did not look, act, or dress like church folk. There were opinions around the table that the church leaders did what they were supposed to do. "He had no business coming up in there untidy and unfit and smoking."

As we sat around the dinner table, about ten of us children and my parents, my father said to us, "That man fits the description of all of us." In his simple theology and rich faith in Christ, he passionately told us about who Jesus came to save

> *For when we were still without strength, in due time Christ died for the ungodly.* [7] *For scarcely for a righteous man will one die; yet perhaps for a good man someone would even dare to die.* [8] *But God demonstrates His own love toward us, in that while we were still sinners, Christ died for us (Romans 5:6-8).*

My father told us that no one in the sanctuary that day had "no business being there." Every person in that place was unfit, untidy, uncombed, un-shaven, poor hygiene and deserved to be expelled. All of us stink when we get close to Jesus. Everyone in there that day was a stranger to the family of God. The only thing that made us a little different or perhaps, a big different was Grace. Our hair was not combed enough, we were not clean enough and in spite of the sharp clothing that was being worn, we were all hobos, vagabonds wondering in a desert land…STRANGERS.

The Afro American church has been, for the Afro American community, something more than a holy place where the people come to learn more about and to be near God. It has served as a social center where fellowship and relationship with family and neighbors have been nurtured. It has also been a place where Afro-Americans could dress with the latest fashions and footwear, sharp dresses, colorful suits and ties, big hats and fine jewelry. If you really wanted to see the latest fashions and designs, the sharpest outfit or the sharpest car or the latest hair-dos that are worn and driven by black people, just go to church.

Some years ago, I attempted to witness to a young man and encourage him to bring his family to church on Sunday. He said to me that he could not compete with church-folk fashions. "Pastor, I am struggling very hard to put food on my family's table and keep clothes on my children's backs. It would be a waste for me to buy clothes just for going to church. He was right. In many churches, he would be a strange fish. The other fish would treat him differently and in some instances, look down on him.

In this post-modern world of cultures and counter-cultures, sometimes in hostile opposition with one another, how should the church deal with fish that do not look like those in the cooler or in the live-well? How should the church treat and encounter the strange fish that happen to get on the hook? Should we be afraid to touch? Should they be treated like they are poison? Should we throw them back? Yes, back to the devil, back to a life of sin and degradation simply because they look different.

Jesus said:

> *I have other sheep that are not of this fold. I must bring them in as well, and they will listen to My voice. Then there will be one flock and one shepherd (John 10:16).*

In John 21, in the wake and aftermath of the Crucifixion, the distraught disciples have decided to return to what they were doing before Jesus called them to discipleship. After a long night of fishing, they again had not caught any fish. In the early morning hours, Jesus appeared and shouted out to them, "Have you caught any fish?" They responded "No."

> *(John 21:6KJV) And he said unto them, Cast the net on the right side of the ship, and ye shall find. They cast therefore, and now they were not able to draw it for the multitude of fishes.*

> *(John 21:10-11) Jesus saith unto them, Bring of the fish which ye have now caught. Simon Peter went up, and drew the net to land full of great fishes, an hundred and fifty and three: and for all there were so many, yet was not the net broken.*

In all of the other versions that I checked, instead of using the word "fishes" like King James did, the word "fish" is used.

Fish vs. fishes

*The plural of fish is usually **fish**, but **fishes** has a few uses. In biology, for instance, fishes is used to refer to **multiple species of fish**. For example, if you say you saw four fish when scuba diving, that means you saw four individual fish, but if you say you saw four fishes, we might infer that you saw an undetermined number of fish of four different species.*

I would like to interpret this verse in the context of "fishes" and not just "fish." Fish means that they are all alike. "Fishes" mean that there are more than one kind of fish. There were all kinds in the net. Not once do we see they threw any back. They counted them (153), meaning that they touched every one of them. They acknowledged their worth by giving each a "number" recognition.

The kind of folk that once filled the pews is diminishing every day. The new kid on the church block is a stranger to the old pew. They do not look like the native church folk, they do not wear what the native church folk wear, their hair-dos are different and their fashions are strangely designed. We were not allowed to wear those clothes in the public when we were young.

The churches who are dead set on maintaining the kind of church that mama approved and disregard the strangers who are getting caught in the net too, those churches who keep throwing back the strange fish without considering making them a part of the catch, those churches that see the un-churched as being unfit and poison, will soon cease to exist. The challenge for the forward-thinking church leaders is to find ways to welcome and embrace non-traditional people into the catch. These are people who do not fit the mode and description of "church folk." The native fish must begin to love and embrace and accept the strange fish (the immigrant fish).

Perhaps the reason why I have been getting so many hits by this strange fish is because the fishermen have been throwing them back. We keep complaining that the church is dying and that the pews are getting emptier and emptier. It maybe that we have reserved the pew for the dead. It may be that we have not come to realize that mama and auntee have left us and gone home. They do not need their seats anymore. It is a perfect time to offer them to the strange fish. Yes, for the traditional fisherman, they take a bit of getting used to but I have discovered that they even taste better once you get past the myths, the misunderstanding, the differences and the suspicions.

What should we do to get started?

1. Dress Down

Choose Sundays that members can dress casual. Wear clothing that is worn every day to school, to work, to dinner, etc. Have them invite others; family, friends, neighbors, coworkers, etc., who are un-churched. Have them wear the same kind of clothing. Ask members not to wear expensive or designer fashions, suits and ties. Leave the big hats in the box and the shiny rocks on the dresser. Make the strangers feel comfortable. Give them a sense of belonging and convey to them that they are not different. Be sure to have the leaders and big-shots lead the way.

2. Do Not Segregate

When you catch them, do not put them in a different live well. Integrate them in the same ministries that all the others are in, including leadership such as deacons, deaconesses, choirs, hostesses, hospitality and youth. Be sure that they are oriented in discipleship, emphasizing the power of prayer and the Lordship of Christ. Assign long time members to mentor, pray and partner with them. Be sure that they are not left out of the news and activities that are so often limited to the native fish.

3. Develop Relationships

Spend time listening, communicating and engaging the strange fish. Move quickly to move them from new-member status to "one of us." Reach out to their family and show interest in their ideas and perspectives. Send personal letters and greeting cards on special days. Avoid condemning words and stories that might make them think you are specifically talking to or about them.

4. Go After the Missing

I caught five of those strange fish last Friday but I hooked about ten. They got off! I was very disappointed and after getting another lure on the line, I went back after them.

The strange fish is hard to hook and even harder to keep. Perhaps it is because I am not use to catching its kind. The church stranger is like the strange fish, "hard to catch and keep." The church ought to have a system in place that will go after the stranger when they go missing. While this can be challenging, it is in keeping with what Jesus would have us do.

> *What man of you, having a hundred sheep, if he loses one of them, does not leave the ninety-nine in the wilderness, and go after the one which is lost until he finds it? And when he has found it, he lays it on his shoulders, rejoicing. And when he comes home, he calls together his friends and neighbors, saying to them, "Rejoice with me, for I have found my sheep which was lost!" (Luke 15:4-6)*

5. Use their Testimonies to Evangelize

Fish of the same species know how to talk to each other. Create environments that encourage strange fish to share their faith experiences and their encounters with the savior.

John 25:31-40

> *When the Son of Man comes in His glory, and all the holy angels with Him, then He will sit on the throne*

of His glory. ³² All the nations will be gathered before Him, and He will separate them one from another, as a shepherd divides his sheep from the goats. ³³ And He will set the sheep on His right hand, but the goats on the left. ³⁴ Then the King will say to those on His right hand, 'Come, you blessed of My Father, inherit the kingdom prepared for you from the foundation of the world: ³⁵ for I was hungry and you gave Me food; I was thirsty and you gave Me drink; I was a stranger and you took Me in; ³⁶ I was naked and you clothed Me; I was sick and you visited Me; I was in prison and you came to Me.'

³⁷ Then the righteous will answer Him, saying, 'Lord, when did we see You hungry and feed You, or thirsty and give You drink? ³⁸ When did we see You a stranger and take You in, or naked and clothe You? ³⁹ Or when did we see You sick, or in prison, and come to You?' ⁴⁰ And the King will answer and say to them, 'Assuredly, I say to you, inasmuch as you did it to one of the least of these My brethren, you did it to Me.'

(Endnotes)

[1] Boiling Point – author: George Barna

[2] Matthews 6:21

[3] Pew Research center – Religious and Public Life. Religion among the Millennials.

[4] Counter Culture – author: David Platt

[5] Your God is too Small – author: J.B. Phillips

[6] Speaking Parables – author: David Buttrick

[7] Pew Research Center, Internet Science and Tech Social network fact Sheet

[8] Matthew Henry Concise Commentary Revelation 2:1-7

[9] The Kind of Preaching God Blesses – Steven J Lawson pg13

[10] The Kind of Preaching God Blesses – Steven J Lawson pg23

[11] (*Apologeticus*, Chapter 50).

[12] Dietrich Bonhoftner - The Cost of Discipleship pg98

[13] The African American Registry – "the Black Church" A Brief History

[14] The African American Registry – "the Black Church" A Brief History

[15] ED Stetzer is president of LifeWay Research and missiologist in residence at LifeWay Christian Resources in Nashville, Tennessee.

[16] Speaking Parables – author: David Buttrick

49120935R00061

Made in the USA
San Bernardino, CA
14 May 2017